D1108134

Let's Talk About

DISOBEYING

Grolier Enterprises Inc. offers a varied selection of both
adult and children's book racks. For details on ordering,
please write: Grolier Enterprises Inc., Sherman Turnpike,
Danbury, CT 06816 Attn: Premium Department

Copyright © 1982 by Joy Berry

No part of this book may be reproduced by any
mechanical, photographic or electronic process, or in
the form of a phonographic recording, nor may it be
stored in a retrieval system, transmitted, or otherwise be
copied for public or private use without the written
permission of the publisher.

Let's Talk About
DISOBEYING

By JOY BERRY

Illustrated by John Costanza
Edited by Orly Kelly
Designed by Jill Losson

GROLIER ENTERPRISES CORP.

Let's talk about DISOBEYING.

When you do not do what your parents ask you to do, you are DISOBEYING them.

Your parents have good reasons for telling you what to do. Therefore, it is not good for you to disobey them.

Your parents tell you what to do because *they do not want you to hurt* yourself or other people.

Your parents tell you what to do because *they do not want you to damage or destroy* your things or other people's things.

Your parents tell you what to do because *they want you to be liked* by other people.

Your parents tell you what to do because *they want you to be fair.*

Parents tell you what to do because they love you and care about the people around you.

Even so, you may sometimes wonder —
• why do my parents get to tell me what to do?
• why can't I tell myself what to do?

It is best that your parents tell you what to do because *they are older and wiser.*

They have lived a lot longer than you. Because they have lived longer, they have learned more.

Because they know more than you, they usually know what is best for you.

It is best that your parents tell you what to do because *they are responsible for you.*

If you do something to hurt yourself or others, your parents may be blamed. They may have to take care of the damage that you have done.

To make sure that you obey them, your parents may need to *punish you* when you disobey.

A punishment will make you feel badly. It will cause you to be sorry for disobeying.

It will make you not want to disobey again.

You might want to do the following so that you will not need to be punished:

- Find out what your parents *want* you to do.
- Find out what your parents *don't want* you to do.
- Listen to your parents. Give them your full attention when they are talking to you.
- Be sure that you understand your parents. Ask them questions if you are not sure you know what they mean.

If you do not agree with your parents, don't nag them or throw a tantrum. Talk with them kindly. Give them some time to think about what you have said.

What you say may cause them to change their minds. If it doesn't, don't talk about it anymore. If you keep talking, you will only frustrate yourself and cause your parents to become angry.

Once you understand what your parents want, *do what they tell you to do*.

If you should occasionally disobey your parents, don't lie about it. Lying will only make things worse.

If you should disobey your parents, there are several things you should do:
- Tell them the truth.
- Tell them that you are sorry (and mean it).
- Accept your punishment. Don't be angry with them; remember, it was you who disobeyed.
- Try not to disobey again.

When you obey your parents, you will please them and you will be doing what is best for yourself.